THE PLANETS

By GAIL GIBBONS

HOLIDAY HOUSE · NEW YORK

For Charlie Pratt

Special thanks to Professor Edward Foley,
teacher of astronomy, St. Michael's College,
Colchester, Vermont

Copyright © 1993 by Gail Gibbons
All rights reserved
Printed in the United States of America
First Edition
Library of Congress Cataloging-in-Publication Data
Gibbons, Gail.
    The planets / by Gail Gibbons.
        p.   cm.
    Summary: Discusses the movements, location, and characteristics
of the nine known planets of our solar system.
    ISBN 0-8234-1040-4
    1. Planets—Juvenile literature. [1. Planets.] I. Title.
QB602.G53   1993   92-44429   CIP   AC
523.4—dc20

PLANET

On a clear night, when stars shine brightly, you might see what looks like another star. But each night it changes position in the star patterns. It is a planet. The word, planet, comes from the Greek word meaning "wanderer."

SUN

PLANET

STAR

A planet is different from a star. People can see a planet because the sun shines on it. A star shines because it is made up of gases that give off light and heat. Our sun is a star. Nearly every star is much bigger than the biggest planet.

In very early times, people knew of six planets. They were Mercury, Venus, Earth, Mars, Jupiter and Saturn. These people named the planets after Greek and Roman goddesses and gods. Later, within the last 200 years, three more were discovered. They are Uranus, Neptune and Pluto.

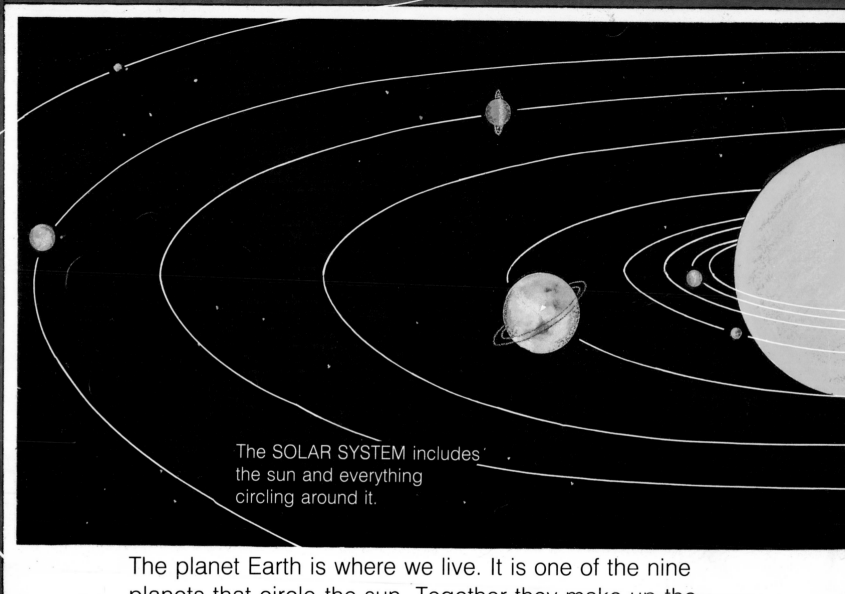

The SOLAR SYSTEM includes the sun and everything circling around it.

The planet Earth is where we live. It is one of the nine planets that circle the sun. Together they make up the main part of the solar system. The word solar means "connected to the sun."

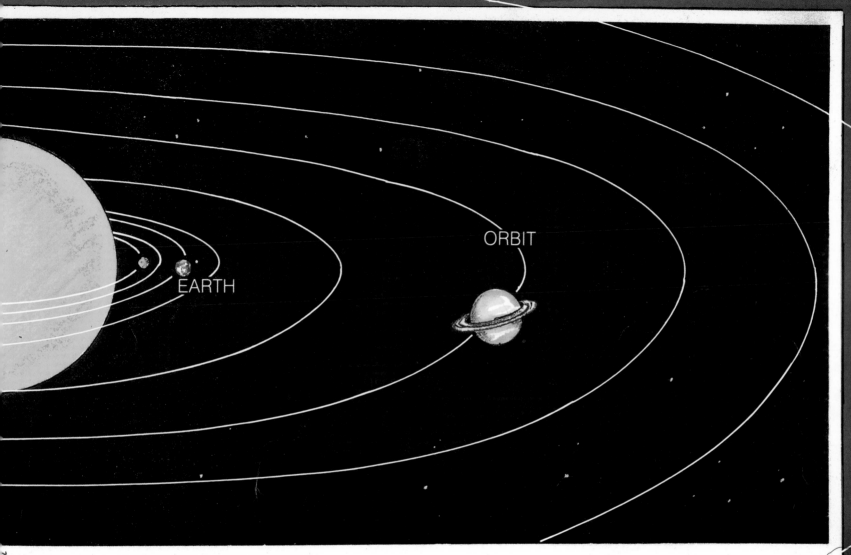

ORBIT

EARTH

The nine planets circle around the sun in paths called
orbits. The time it takes for a planet to travel around the
sun is its year. Each planet's year is different.

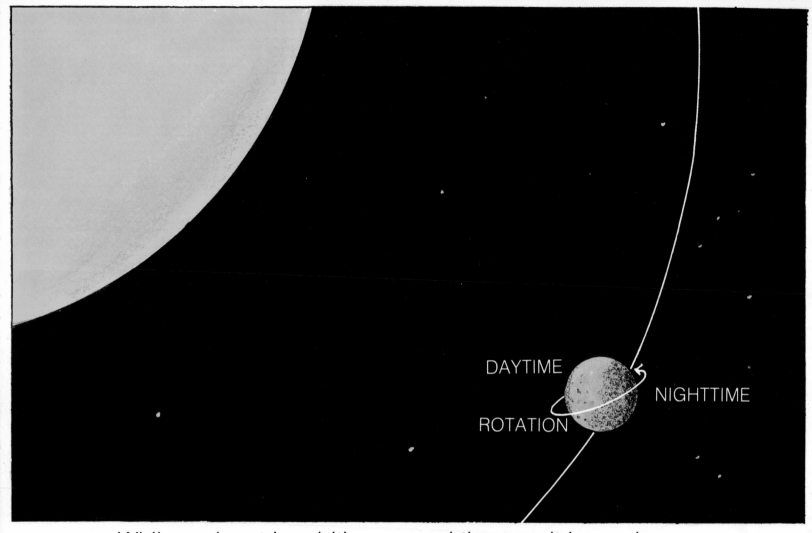

DAYTIME

NIGHTTIME

ROTATION

While a planet is orbiting around the sun, it is moving another way, too. It spins, or rotates. The time it takes for a planet to rotate is its day. Each planet's day is different. While a planet is rotating, part of it faces the sun. It is daytime there. On the other side it is nighttime.

A TELESCOPE enlarges the image.

People can look up on a clear night and might see Mercury, Venus, Mars, Jupiter and Saturn. A planet looks like a steady point of light. A star twinkles. A telescope is needed to see Uranus, Neptune and Pluto. They are very far away from planet Earth.

MERCURY

An ATMOSPHERE is
a layer of air.

MERCURY

Of the nine planets, Mercury is the planet closest to the
sun. It is about 36 million miles away from the sun.
During the day it is extremely hot. During the night, it is
bitter cold because Mercury doesn't have any
atmosphere to keep its heat from escaping.

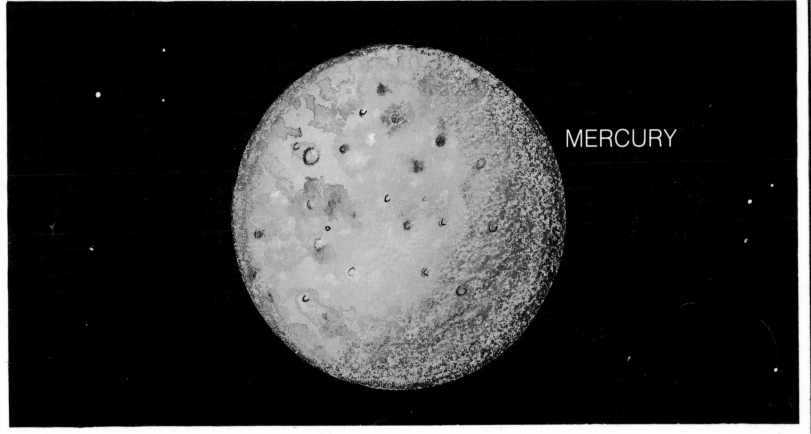

MERCURY

Mercury is the second smallest planet of the nine
planets and is made up of rock and metal. One year on
Mercury is only 88 Earth days. That's how long it takes
for Mercury to orbit the sun. Mercury rotates very
slowly, so its days are very long. A day on Mercury is
59 Earth days.

VENUS

●VENUS

Venus is the second planet from the sun. It is the brightest object in our sky, other than our sun and moon. At sunrise and sunset, it looks like a big, bright star. It is bright because Venus has a cloud cover that reflects the sunlight. These clouds are made up of gases.

MERCURY

VENUS

Venus is about 67 million miles away from the sun. It is hot there. Venus is almost the same size as planet Earth. One year on Venus is about 225 Earth days. A day on Venus is about 243 Earth days long because it rotates very slowly. So on Venus, a day is longer than a year, and a year is shorter than a day.

EARTH

Earth is the third planet from the sun. It is the only planet known to have just the right environment for plants, animals and people to live in. Earth is 93 million miles from the sun.

A MOON orbits a planet. It has no light of its own. It reflects sunlight.

EARTH

GRAVITY pulls things toward Earth.

VENUS

MERCURY

The planet Earth has just enough gravity to hold its atmosphere around it. Earth has a moon. The moon causes the tides to change, making them rise and fall. Earth orbits the sun in about 365 days to make an Earth year. It rotates every 24 hours to make an Earth day.

MARS

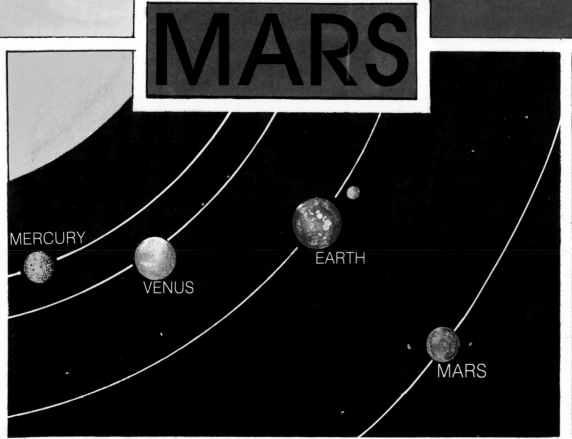

VIKING
SPACECRAFT

MERCURY

VENUS

EARTH

MARS

Mars is the fourth planet from the sun, about 142 million miles away. At one time, people thought there might be creatures, called Martians, and other life forms on this planet. They saw dusty lines and patterns on Mars's surface. People thought they might be canals. In 1976, two Viking spacecraft visited Mars. There was no sign of life.

MARS

Astronomers believe that Mars looks red because iron on its surface has been rusted by the planet's thin atmosphere. It is very cold and is a little more than half the size of planet Earth. Mars has two small moons. One year on Mars is about two Earth years. A day on Mars is about as long as a day on Earth.

JUPITER

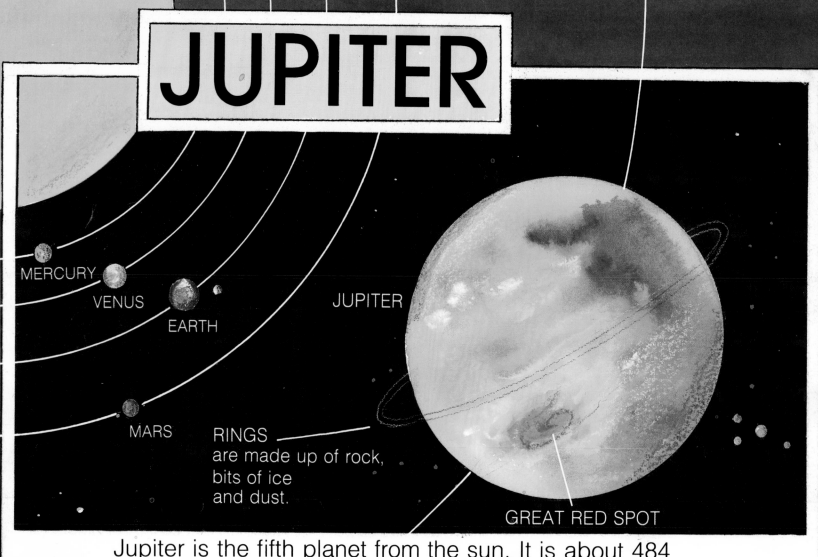

MERCURY

VENUS

EARTH

MARS

JUPITER

RINGS
are made up of rock,
bits of ice
and dust.

GREAT RED SPOT

Jupiter is the fifth planet from the sun. It is about 484 million miles away. It is huge! It is bigger than all the other planets put together and has rings. Jupiter is mostly made up of gases. Some of the gases form a giant red circle called the Great Red Spot.

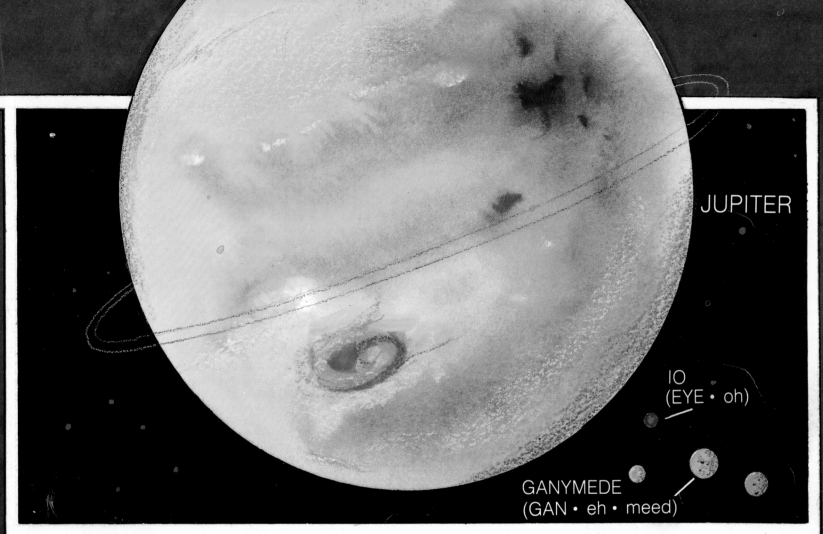

JUPITER

IO
(EYE • oh)

GANYMEDE
(GAN • eh • meed)

At least 16 moons orbit around the planet Jupiter. One moon, Ganymede, is the biggest moon in the solar system. It is bigger than the planet Mercury. Another moon, called Io, has many active volcanoes. One Jupiter year is almost 12 Earth years. It has short days, just under ten Earth hours long.

SATURN

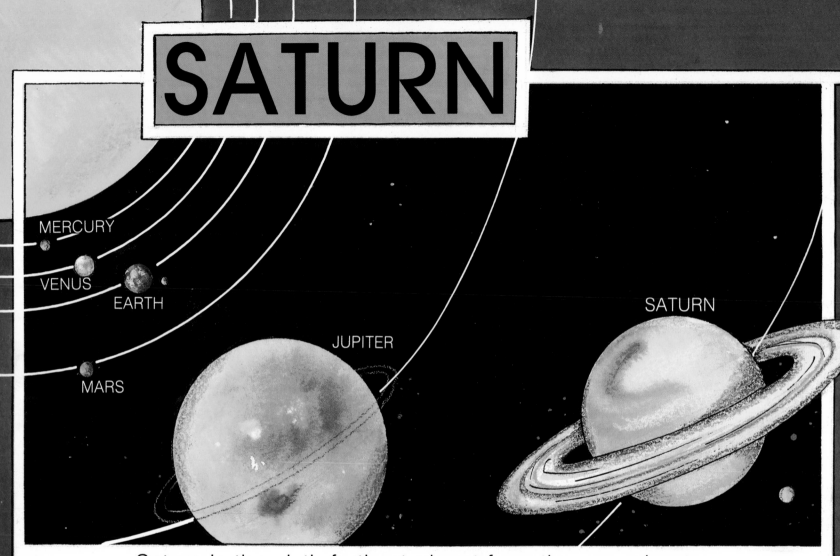

MERCURY

VENUS

EARTH

MARS

JUPITER

SATURN

Saturn is the sixth farthest planet from the sun, about
887 million miles away. It is the second largest planet.
Saturn's hundreds of rings make it look different from
the other planets. The rings are made up of rock, bits
of ice and dust. On Saturn it is extremely cold.

SATURN

TITAN
(TITE · n)

Saturn has at least 24 moons, more than any other planet. Titan, its largest moon, is the only moon in the solar system with an atmosphere and clouds. It takes almost 30 Earth years for Saturn to orbit the sun. It rotates in about 11 Earth hours.

URANUS

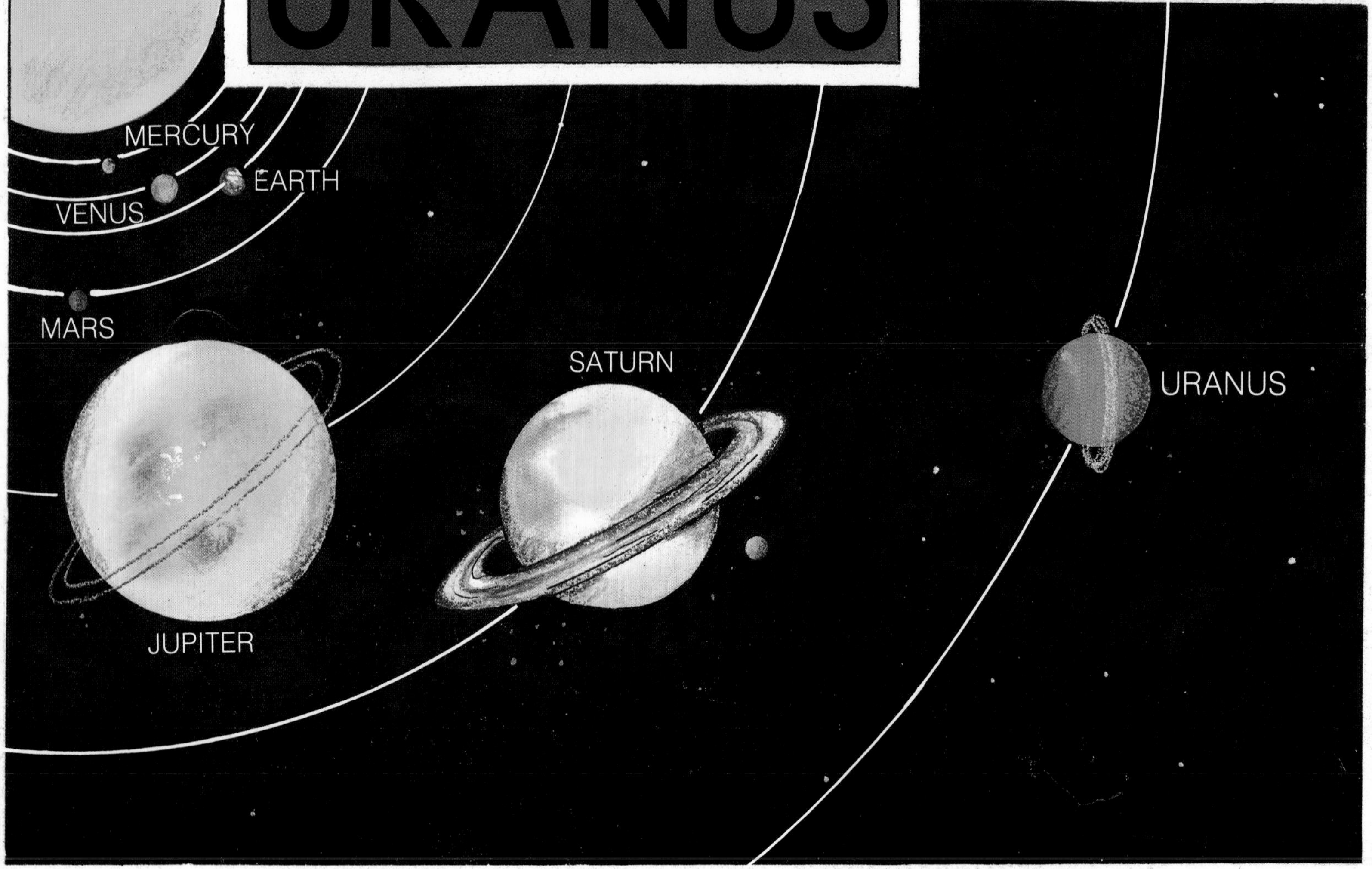

MERCURY

VENUS

EARTH

MARS

JUPITER

SATURN

URANUS

Uranus is the seventh planet from the sun. It is about 1.8 billion miles away. It is so far away that from its surface the sun would look tiny. Uranus has ten rings.

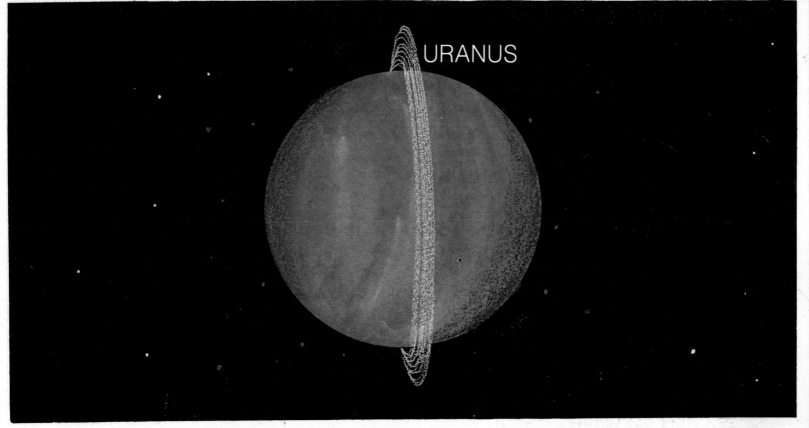

URANUS

Uranus is the third biggest planet, about one third the size of the planet Jupiter. At least 15 moons orbit around it. Planets farther from the sun have longer orbits. They take more time to travel around the sun. For Uranus, to make one orbit takes about 84 Earth years. Uranus rotates in about 17 Earth hours.

NEPTUNE

MERCURY
VENUS EARTH
MARS
JUPITER
SATURN
URANUS
NEPTUNE

Neptune is the eighth farthest planet from the sun. It is about 2.8 billion miles away. Neptune appears to be blue because of a gas in its atmosphere. It is almost the same size as Uranus.

One of Neptune's eight moons, Triton, is about the same size as the planet Earth's moon. The spacecraft, *Voyager II,* visited Neptune in 1989. One Neptune year is 164 Earth years. It rotates in about 16 Earth hours.

PLUTO

MERCURY
VENUS
EARTH
MARS
JUPITER
SATURN
URANUS

Pluto usually is the ninth and farthest planet from the sun. Sometimes its orbit carries it closer to the sun than Neptune. At its farthest, Pluto is about 3.6 billion miles from the sun. It was discovered in 1930.

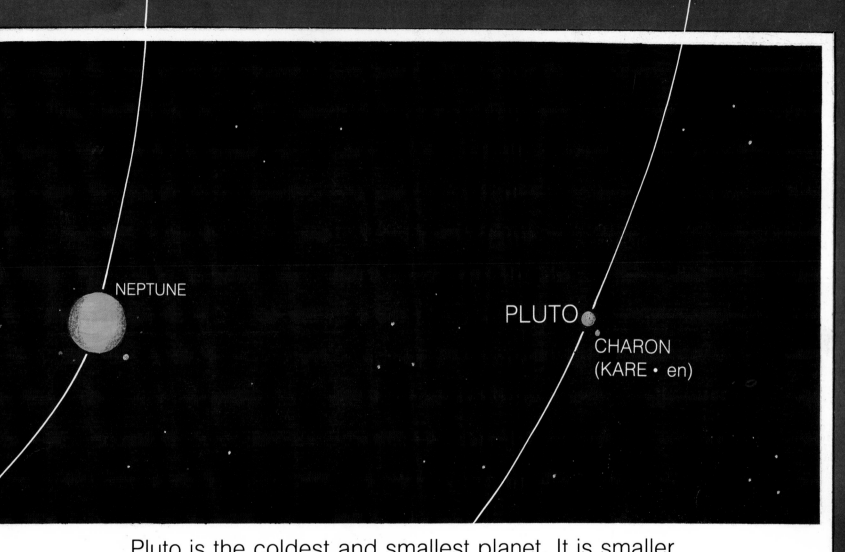

NEPTUNE

PLUTO

CHARON
(KARE • en)

Pluto is the coldest and smallest planet. It is smaller
than the Earth's moon. It has one moon called Charon.
One year on Pluto is about 248 Earth years long. A day
on Pluto is about six Earth days long.

An ASTRONOMER is someone who studies the stars and planets.

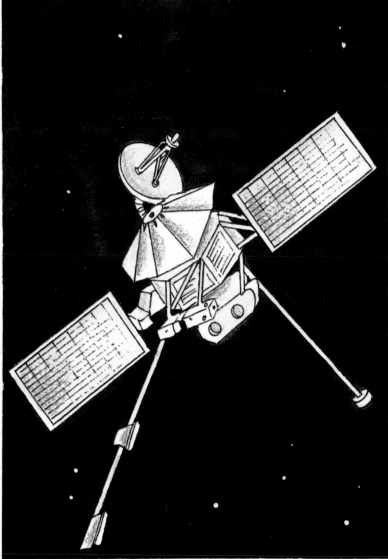

Here on planet Earth, astronomers search the skies through telescopes. Spacecraft are sent into the solar system and beyond in search of new discoveries.

We are always learning about the planets, the stars and
what lies beyond. It is fun to search the night skies for
planets and stars from our planet Earth.

MORE ABOUT OUR NINE PLANETS

MERCURY

Mercury, which is slightly bigger than the Earth's moon, has a core of iron.

VENUS

Venus rotates in the opposite direction of the other eight planets.

EARTH

Earth is the middle-sized planet. Four of the nine planets are smaller and four are bigger than the planet Earth.

MARS

Mars has a very large canyon. It is the biggest in the solar system. It is called Mariner Valley and is thirteen times longer than the Grand Canyon in the United States.

JUPITER

Jupiter is huge! If Jupiter were a big, empty ball, over 1,000 Earths would fill it.

SATURN

It is very windy on Saturn. Around its middle, winds blow ten times stronger than an average hurricane on Earth.

URANUS

When the spacecraft, *Voyager II*, flew past Uranus in 1986, it had been traveling through space for nine years.

NEPTUNE

Neptune is thirty times Earth's distance from the sun. Some astronomers have said that studying Neptune from Earth is like studying a dime a mile away.

PLUTO

Some astronomers think that Pluto is an escaped moon from Neptune or another planet.